Weather Changes in a Flash

CONTENTS

NATIONAL GEOGRAPHIC
School Publishing
Hampton-Brown

i

_ie

_igh

Words with i, ie, igh

Look at each picture. Read the words.

Example:

p**ie**

h**i**!

n**igh**t

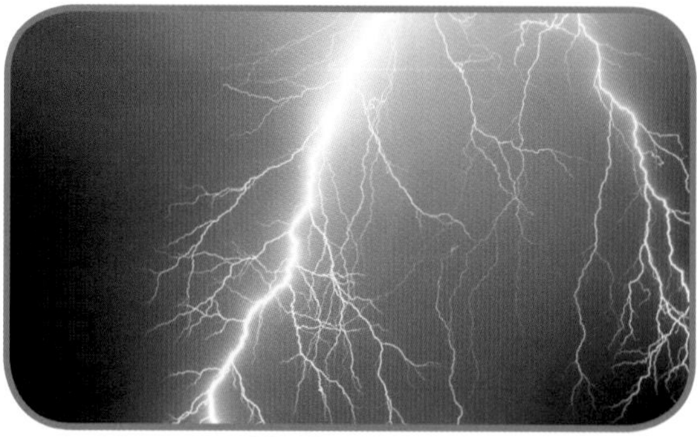

l**igh**tning

t**ie**

p**i**lot

High Frequency Words
air
earth
even
hear
here
morning
near
round
sound
start

Key Words

Look at the pictures. Read Jake's note to his mom.

I sleep here.

We had a lightning show!

Dear Mom,

Things **here** at camp are fine. You can see that I sleep **near** the lake. This **morning** we had a light show in the **air**. There was lightning, as you can see. Not one stroke hit the **earth**. I wish you could **hear** the **sound**, too!

We are about to **start** a fun game. We toss a beanbag **round** and round. We cannot drop it. I might **even** win!

I miss you,
Jake

Phonics Games
NGReach.com

Lightning!

by Deanne W. Kells

You see big, thick clouds in the sky. Then the rain starts. Flash! You see lightning. Next, you hear a big clap of thunder. Are you filled with fright or delight?

Lightning is quite a sight. It can light up the sky. It is quick, strong, and hot.

What is lightning? It is a flash of electricity. Air and water go round and round in a cloud. Hot and cold air get all mixed up. Things get wild in the cloud. Then, bam! Electricity!

A lightning stroke is fast. It can take a zigzag path. It can split into branches. Lightning can even look like a string of cotton lumps or beads.

Lightning is silent. But it heats up the air and smashes it into a sound wave. That wave makes the crash of thunder that you hear.

Lightning might start in a cloud and stay there. It might jump to the next cloud. It might streak down and strike land. That is why people need to be safe when there is lightning.

If lightning strikes you, its electricity will shock you. Stay inside when there is lightning. But do not take a bath or use electricity.

Why is it safe inside, even in high buildings? These buildings have lightning rods. A lightning rod can catch electricity. It sends it right into the earth.

If you are out and there is lightning, get to low land. High land and land near water are not safe. Stay low but do not lie flat. Wait for the crisis to pass—when the lightning has stopped.

You can see more lightning flashes from twilight on than in daylight. The bright flashes light up the night sky!

Lightning will not last long. It ends, and the clouds pass by. It's hard to think there was lightning here this morning! ❖

Words with i, ie, igh

Read these words.

bright	die	hot	night	silent
delight	high	midnight	safe	white

Find the words with **i**, **ie**, or **igh**. Use letters to build them.

d e l i g h t

Talk Together

Choose words from the box above to tell your partner facts about lightning.

The lightning at midnight is high.

Words with
kn, gn, wr, mb

Look at each picture. Read the words.

Example:

knot

la**mb**

gnome

si**gn**

thu**mb**

write

High Frequency Words
air
earth
even
hear
here
morning
near
round
sound
start

Key Words

Look at the pictures. Read the sentences.

A May Day Pole

Do you feel spring in the **air**? Do you **hear** the **sound** of spring? Can you **even** smell spring? Make a May Day pole to say, "Spring is **here**!"

1. **Start** by knocking the pole into the **earth**.
2. Tape bright strips **near** the top.
3. On the **morning** of May Day, grab a strip. Go **round** and round the pole.

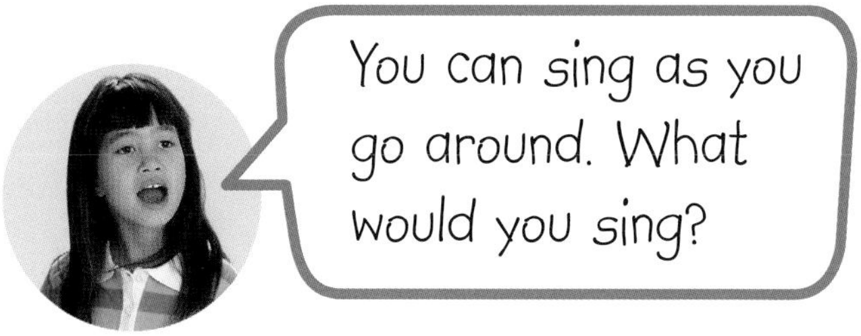

Phonics Games
NGReach.com

Signs of Spring

by Tae Choi

Some places have long winters. People might not like all the snow. They might not like numb noses and toes.

But winter will not last all year! What are some signs that spring is on its way? Let's use our senses to find them.

You can hear a morning sound that means spring is here. It is the sound of birds singing. Some birds greet sunrise with a song.

Some birds go to warm places for the winter. They come back for the spring. The sweet morning-song of a wren can mean spring is near.

Use the sense of sight to find signs of spring. Look for plump, round buds on a tree limb. Or look for green plants poking out of the earth.

Look for young animals like lambs or tadpoles. Spring is a fine time for plants and animals to grow!

If you have a knack for growing things, plant them in spring. We say that people who can grow things well have a "green thumb."

You can feel spring in the air. It gets warm! When you are out, you do not need to wrap up in a thick coat. You can use a light jacket.

Some people say their backs or knees let them know that spring is here. They get pains from the cold of winter. In spring, the pains stop. Things that felt wrong start to feel right!

Some people say they can even smell spring. They smell the fresh rain. They smell the flowers.

Do you think you can taste spring? When a knife cuts fresh fruit, you can smell it and taste it! ❖

Words with <u>kn</u>, <u>gn</u>, <u>wr</u>, <u>mb</u>

Read these words.

bench	limb	knife	pump	wren
lamb	gnome	path	sign	plate

Find the words with **kn**, **gn**, **wr**, or **mb**. Use letters to build them.

g n o m e

Talk Together

Choose words from the box above to tell your partner what you see in spring on the farm.

I see a wren on a limb.

What Am I?

Look at the pictures with a partner. Take turns reading the clues. Then solve the riddle.

1 You can see me at night.
You can see me in daylight.

2 I start up high but can end down on earth.

3 I cut like a knife through the air.

4 I am silent. But a crashing sound you hear is a sign that I am near.

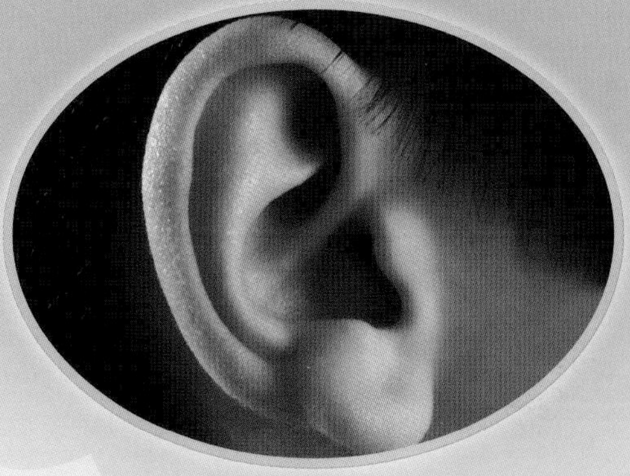

5 I am hot and strong. I can wreck things. I might snap a limb off a tree. I can shock people.

6 You must know that it is wrong to lie flat if I am near.

Answer: I am lightning.

Acknowledgments
Grateful acknowledgment is given to the authors, artists, photographers, museums, publishers, and agents for permission to reprint copyrighted material. Every effort has been made to secure the appropriate permission. If any omissions have been made or if corrections are required, please contact the Publisher.

Photographic Credits
CVR Creatas/Jupiterimages. **2** (bl) Nikolay Okhitin/Shutterstock. (br) Digital Vision/Photodisc/Getty Images. (cl) Soubrette/iStockphoto. (cr) PhotoDisc/Getty Images. (tl) Radius Images/Masterfile. (tr) John Stuart/Alamy Images. **3** (bl) Liz Garza Williams/Hampton-Brown/National Geographic School Publishing. (l) Susan Van Etten/PhotoEdit. (r) Corey Hochachka/age fotostock. **4** Eyewire. **5** Pindyurin Vasily/Shutterstock. **7** (bg) Jhaz Photography/Shutterstock. (inset) Andy Nixon. **9** yuri4u80/Shutterstock. **10** pzAxe/Shutterstock. **11** Melody Mulligan/Shutterstock. **13** Jeremy Woodhouse/PhotoDisc/Getty Images. **14** Digital Vision/Getty Images. **15** (b) Sam Barricklow/Workbook Stock/Getty Images. (r) Liz Garza Williams/Hampton-Brown/National Geographic School Publishing. **16** (bl) Lushpix Stock Images/Unlisted Images, Inc. (br) John Clines/iStockphoto. (cbr) Image Farm/Jupiterimages. (cl) John de la Bastide/Shutterstock. (ctr) Fedor Selivanov/Shutterstock. (tl) Photodisc/Getty Images. **17** (b) Liz Garza Williams/Hampton-Brown/National Geographic School Publishing. **18** Visions of America, LLC/Alamy Images. **19** Andrey Ukhov/Shutterstock. **20** Michael Woodruff/Shutterstock. **21** SuperStock/Alamy Images. **22** (b) Noam Armonn/Shutterstock. (t) Smit/Shutterstock. **23** (b) Albert Lleal/Minden Pictures/National Geographic Image Collection. (t) Fedor Selivanov/Shutterstock. **24** Bill Sykes/Cultura/Alamy Images. **25** (b) Siede Preis/Photodisc/Alamy Images. (cb) Lara Barrett/Shutterstock. (ct) Natallia Bokach/iStockphoto. (t) Tereshchenko Dmitry/Shutterstock. **26** HBSS/Corbis. **27** Olga Perevalova/Shutterstock. **28** (bc, br) Iconotec. (t) Digital Vision/Getty Images. **29** Liz Garza Williams/Hampton-Brown/National Geographic School Publishing. **30** (b) roadk/Shutterstock. (c) Eyewire. (tl) Digital Vision/Getty Images. (tr) Borislav Gnjidic/iStockphoto. **31** (b) Nadzeya Kizilava/Shutterstock. (c) Jonathan Lenz/Shutterstock. (t) aleksandar zoric/Shutterstock.

Illustrator Credits
6, 8, 11, 17, 29 Dartmouth Publishing

National Geographic School Publishing
Hampton-Brown
www.NGSP.com

Printed in the USA.
Quad Graphics, Leominster, MA

ISBN: 978-0-7362-8072-3

17 18 19
10 9 8 7 6 5